CONTENTS

HOW TO MAKE THE BEST ICE CREAM AT HOME

You might be asking how do you make the best home made ice cream? Or how do you scoop the perfect ice cream? Ice Cream Maker Guru has all the tips and tricks to make the perfect home made ice cream.

TIPS FOR WORKING WITH YOUR ICE CREAM MAKER

Top 5 Tips for How to Use Your Ice Cream Maker

1. Preparation is Key
No matter what type of ice cream maker you have, preparation is important. Always remember – a pre-freeze bowl needs to be in the freezer overnight to ensure it is frozen solid. If you can, keep your bowl in the freezer permanently so it is always ready when you need it.
If the bowl is not frozen enough there is a good chance your ice cream won't freeze.

2. Fill Your Ice Cream Maker to the Perfect Spot
Remember that you should not overfill your ice cream maker – about three quarters full is plenty! It might not look like much but filling it to the top can affect the aeration of the ice cream.

3. Have Your Ice Cream Machine Ready to Go
Ensure the motor of your ice cream machine is on before pouring your mixture into the freezer bowl. This will prevent your mixture from immediately freezing.

4. Don't be Chunky! Little Bits are Just Fine!
Your ice cream isn't a food processor so don't expect it to chop and refine chunky ingredients. Add your mix ins such as chocolate chips or nuts towards the end. The last minute or two is plenty of time to distribute your mix ins evenly.

5. Your Ice Cream Machine Deserves Some TLC
Once you have produced some delicious ice cream, you must remember to look after your machine. Wash all your accessories, paddles and lids according to the manufacturers advice.

Ensure your ice cream bowl is set aside to defrost thoroughly BEFORE plunging into hot water. This can damage your bowl beyond repair so please be careful!

SIMPLE ICE CREAM

Blueberry Honey Cake Batter Soft Serve Ice Cream

Servings: 6
Cooking Time: 35 Minutes

Ingredients:

- 2 cups heavy cream
- 1 cup milk
- 3⁄4 cup sugar
- 1 Tbs. vanilla extract
- 2/3 cup cake mix
- ½ cup blueberries
- 2 tablespoons honey

Directions:

1. NOTE: Freeze your ice cream bowl for at least 24hrs prior to starting!
2. Place the milk and cream in a bowl, and mix them together until well combined. Use a whisk to mix in the sugar. Continue to whisk for about 4 minutes until the sugar dissolves. Mix in the vanilla extract, and then the 2/3 cup cake mix honey and blueberries.
3. Pour the ingredients into your ice cream maker, and let it churn for 25 minutes.
4. Serve immediately.

"georgia Peach" Maple Syrup Soft Serve Ice Cream

Servings: 6
Cooking Time: 35 Minutes

Ingredients:

- 2 cups heavy cream
- 1 cup milk
- 3⁄4 cup sugar
- 1 Tbs. vanilla extract
- 1 cup peaches
- ¼ cup maple syrup

Directions:

1. NOTE: Freeze your ice cream bowl for at least 24hrs prior to starting!
2. Puree the peaches in a food processor or blender.
3. Place the milk and cream in a bowl, and mix them together until well combined. Use a whisk to mix in the sugar. Continue to whisk for about 4 minutes until the sugar dissolves. Then mix in the vanilla extract. Then mix in the blueberries, and maple syrup.
4. Pour the ingredients into your ice cream maker, and let it churn for 25 minutes.
5. Serve immediately.

Thermomix Licorice Ice Cream

Servings: 12
Cooking Time: 30 Minutes

Ingredients:

- 3 cups heavy cream
- 2 cups whole milk
- ½ cup sugar
- A pinch of salt
- 6 egg yolks
- ½ teaspoon black food coloring
- ¼ cup soft licorice, chopped

Directions:

1. Add the cream, milk, sugar, and salt in a saucepan and heat over medium low flame. Simmer for 3 minutes or until the sugar dissolves. Remove from the stove.
2. In a bowl, whisk in the egg yolks. Drizzle ½ cup of the warm milk into the egg yolks while whisking constantly to form a smooth mixture. Whisk the egg mixture back into the pot. Add the black food coloring and licorice.
3. Turn on the heat to medium low and cook until the mixture starts to thicken. Constantly stir while cooking.
4. Turn off the heat and strain the mixture to remove lumps. Allow the milk to cool at room temperature. Place in the fridge to chill for 2 hours.
5. Turn on the Cuisinart and pour the mixture in. Churn for 15 minutes.
6. Transfer to an airtight container.
7. Place in the fridge to completely cool.

Nutrition:

- Info Calories per serving342 ; Protein 3g; Carbs 32g; Fat 22g Sugar 22g

Double Espresso Ice Cream

Servings: 10
Cooking Time: 30 Minutes

Ingredients:

- 2 cups half and half
- 1 ½ cups heavy cream
- 14 ounces sweetened condensed milk
- 2 tablespoons espresso powder
- 6 egg yolks
- ¼ cup chocolate-covered espresso beans, chopped

Directions:

1. Add the half and half, cream, condensed milk, and espresso powder in a saucepan and heat over medium low flame. Simmer for 3 minutes. Remove from the stove.
2. In a bowl, whisk in the egg yolks. Drizzle ½ cup of the warm milk into the egg yolks while whisking constantly to form a smooth mixture. Whisk the egg mixture back into the pot.
3. Turn on the heat to medium low and cook until the mixture starts to thicken. Constantly stir while cooking.
4. Turn off the heat and strain the mixture to remove lumps. Allow to cool at room temperature. Place in the fridge to chill for 2 hours.
5. Turn on the Cuisinart and pour the mixture in. Churn for 15 minutes.
6. Five minutes before the time ends, add the chocolate-covered espresso beans.
7. Transfer to an airtight container.
8. Place in the fridge to completely cool.

Nutrition:

- Info Calories per serving:166 ; Protein: 4.8g; Carbs: 9.2g; Fat: 12.4g Sugar: 5.6g

Custard Cantaloupe Ice Cream

Servings: 10
Cooking Time: 30 Minutes

Ingredients:

- 3 cups whole milk
- 1 cup sugar
- 8 egg yolks
- A pinch of salt
- 1 cup cantaloupe, seeds removed and mashed

Directions:

1. Add the milk and sugar in a saucepan and heat over medium low flame. Simmer for 3 minutes or until the sugar dissolves. Remove from the heat.
2. In a bowl, whisk in the egg yolks. Drizzle ½ cup of the warm milk into the egg yolks while whisking constantly to form a smooth mixture. Whisk the egg mixture back into the pot. Add the salt.
3. Turn on the heat to medium low and cook until the mixture starts to thicken. Constantly stir while cooking.
4. Turn off the heat and strain the mixture to remove lumps. Allow the milk to cool at room temperature. Place in the fridge to chill for 2 hours.
5. Turn on the Cuisinart and pour the mixture in. Churn for 15 minutes.
6. Five minutes before the time ends, add the mashed cantaloupe.
7. Transfer to an airtight container.
8. Place in the fridge to completely cool.

Nutrition:

- Info Calories per serving:155 ; Protein: 4.5g; Carbs: 21.4g; Fat: 5.9g Sugar: 20.1g

Blackberry Ice Cream

Servings: 10
Cooking Time: 45 Minutes

Ingredients:

- 1 ½ cups blackberries, frozen or fresh
- ¾ cup ice cold whole milk
- ½ cup sugar
- A pinch of salt
- 1 ½ cup heavy cream, ice cold
- 1 ½ teaspoon vanilla

Directions:

1. Clean the blackberries by removing the stem and seeds. Mash to release the juice and pass through a sieve. Save the juice and set aside.
2. Put ice water in a large mixing bowl. Place a small bowl on top of the large bowl with ice.
3. Place the whole milk, sugar, and salt. Whisk to combine everything. Add the cream, vanilla, and blackberry juice. Stir to combined.
4. Turn on the Cuisinart and pour the mixture in. Freeze for 45 minutes.
5. Transfer into air-tight containers.
6. Freeze overnight.

Nutrition:

- Info Calories per serving: 151; Protein: 3g; Carbs: 15g; Fat: 9.1g Sugar: 13.1g

S'mores Camp Fire Frozen Yogurt

Servings: 1 Quart
Cooking Time: 2 Hours 35 Minutes

Ingredients:

- 1 quart container full-fat plain yogurt
- ¼ teaspoon salt
- 1 cup sugar
- 1 teaspoon vanilla extract
- 3 large graham crackers
- 4 ounces chopped semi-sweet chocolate
- ½ cup mini marshmallows
- 1 tsp smoke flavor extract

Directions:

1. NOTE: Freeze your ice cream bowl for at least 24hrs prior to starting!
2. Place the yogurt in a bowl. Use a whisk to mix in the sugar and salt. Continue to whisk for about 4 minutes until the sugar dissolves. Then mix in the vanilla and smoke flavored extract.
3. Place the graham crackers in a food processor, and process until the crackers are no bigger than chocolate chips. If you don't have a food processor place the crackers in a large resealable plastic bag, and seal it shut. Use your hands, a mallet, or a rolling pin to crush the cookies.
4. Pour the ingredients into your ice cream maker, and let it churn for 25 minutes. About 5 minutes before the ice cream is done churning add the chocolate, graham crackers, and marshmallows to your ice cream maker.
5. Put the frozen yogurt in an airtight container and place in the freezer for at least 2 hours, until desired consistency is reached.

Cherry Blueberry Lime Soda Frozen Yogurt

Servings: 1 Quart
Cooking Time: 2 Hours 50 Minutes

Ingredients:

- 1 quart container full-fat plain yogurt
- ¼ teaspoon salt
- 1 cup sugar
- ½ lime (peeled and cut up fine)
- 1/2 cup blueberries
- 1 teaspoon vanilla extract
- 3 cups (2, 12 ounce cans) cherry soda

Directions:

1. NOTE: Freeze your ice cream bowl for at least 24hrs prior to starting!
2. Pour the cherry soda into a large skillet, and heat it on high heat until it comes to a boil. Allow the coke to cook for about another 15 or 20 minutes, until the root beer reduces down to 1 cup of liquid. Let the liquid cool.
3. Place the yogurt in a bowl. Use a whisk to mix in the sugar and salt. Continue to whisk for about 4 minutes until the sugar dissolves. Then mix in the vanilla extract, blueberries, lime and reduced cherry soda.
4. Pour the ingredients into your ice cream maker, and let it churn for 25 minutes.
5. Put the frozen yogurt in an airtight container and place in the freezer for at least 2 hours, until desired consistency is reached.

Cinnamon Chocolate Chip Soft Serve Ice Cream

Servings: 6
Cooking Time: 35 Minutes

Ingredients:

- 2 cups heavy cream
- 1 cup milk
- 3⁄4 cup sugar
- 1 Tbs. vanilla extract
- 1 cup chocolate chips of your choice
- 2 tsps. cinnamon

Directions:

1. NOTE: Freeze your ice cream bowl for at least 24hrs prior to starting!
2. Place the milk and cream in a bowl, and mix them together until well combined. Use a whisk to mix in the sugar. Continue to whisk for about 4 minutes until the sugar dissolves. Then mix in the vanilla extract.
3. Pour the ingredients into your ice cream maker, and let it churn for 25 minutes. About 5 minutes before the ice cream is finished churning, add in the chocolate chips.
4. Serve immediately.

Graham Cracker Peanut Butter Cup Milkshake

Servings: 6
Cooking Time: 25 Minutes

Ingredients:

- 2 cups heavy cream
- 1 cup milk
- 3/4 cup sugar
- 1 tablespoon vanilla extract
- 1 1/2 cups chopped mini peanut butter cups
- ½ cup maple syrup
- 4 graham crackers

Directions:

1. NOTE: Freeze your ice cream bowl for at least 24hrs prior to starting!
2. Place the milk and cream in a bowl, and mix them together until well combined. Use a whisk to mix in the sugar. Continue to whisk for about 4 minutes until the sugar dissolves. Then mix in the vanilla extract.
3. Pour the ingredients into your ice cream maker, and let it churn for 10-15 minutes, until desired consistency is reached. About 5 minutes before the ice cream is done churning add the peanut butter cup and the graham crackers to your ice cream maker.
4. Serve immediately.

Green Apple Musketeer Gelato

Servings: 4-6
Cooking Time: 2 Hours 35 Minutes

Ingredients:

- 1/2 cup heavy cream
- 2 cups milk
- 3/4 cup sugar
- 1 tablespoon vanilla extract
- 1 ½ cups chopped mini Musketeers bars
- ¼ cup green apples

Directions:

1. NOTE: Freeze your ice cream bowl for at least 24hrs prior to starting!
2. Place the milk and cream in a bowl, and mix them together until well combined. Use a whisk to mix in the sugar. Continue to whisk for about 4 minutes until the sugar dissolves. Then mix in the vanilla extract.
3. Pour the ingredients into your ice cream maker, and let it churn for 25 minutes. About 5 minutes before the ice cream is done churning add the three musketeers and green apples to your ice cream maker.
4. Put the gelato in an airtight container and place in the freezer for up to 2 hours, until desired consistency is reached.

Sour Patch Chocolate Ice Cream

Servings: 6
Cooking Time: 2 Hours 50 Minutes

Ingredients:

- 2 cups heavy cream
- 1 cup milk
- 3/4 cup sugar
- 1 tablespoon vanilla extract
- 1 cups chopped sour patch
- ½ cup chocolate (chopped fine)

Directions:

1. NOTE: Freeze your ice cream bowl for at least 24hrs prior to starting!
2. Place the milk and cream in a bowl, and mix them together until well combined. Use a whisk to mix in the sugar. Continue to whisk for about 4 minutes until the sugar dissolves. Then mix in the vanilla extract.
3. Pour the ingredients into your ice cream maker, and let it churn for 25 minutes. About 5 minutes before the ice cream is done churning add the sour patch and chocolate to your ice cream maker.
4. Put the ice cream in an airtight container and place in the freezer for around 2 hours. Allow the ice cream to thaw for 15 minutes before serving.

Cookies 'n Cream Rice Crispy Treat Frozen Yogurt

Servings: 1 Quart
Cooking Time: 2 Hours 35 Minutes

Ingredients:

- 1 quart container full-fat plain yogurt
- ¼ teaspoon salt
- 1 cup sugar
- 1 teaspoon vanilla extract
- 10 chocolate sandwich cookies
- 1/2 cup rice crispy treats

Directions:

1. Refer to note at the beginning of the chapter about freezing bowl.
2. Place the yogurt in a bowl. Use a whisk to mix in the sugar and salt. Continue to whisk for about 4 minutes until the sugar dissolves. Then mix in the vanilla extract.
3. Place the sandwich cookies in a food processor, and process until the cookies are no bigger than chocolate chips. If you don't have a food processor place the cookies in a large resealable plastic bag, and seal it shut. Use your hands, a mallet, or a rolling pin to crush the cookies.
4. Pour the ingredients into your ice cream maker, and let it churn for 25 minutes. About 5 minutes before the ice cream is done churning add the cookies, and small chunks of the rice crispy treats to your ice cream maker.
5. Put the frozen yogurt in an airtight container and place in the freezer for at least 2 hours, until desired consistency is reached.

FRUITILICIOUS ICE CREAM

Bursting Banana Nut Gelato

Servings: 4-6
Cooking Time: 2 Hours 35 Minutes

Ingredients:

- 1/2 cup heavy cream
- 2 cups milk
- 3/4 cup sugar
- 1 tablespoon vanilla extract
- 1 cup sliced banana
- ½ cup chopped walnuts

Directions:

1. Refer to note at the beginning of the chapter about freezing bowl.
2. Puree the bananas in a food processor or blender.
3. Place the milk and cream in a bowl, and mix them together until well combined. Use a whisk to mix in the sugar. Continue to whisk for about 4 minutes until the sugar dissolves. Then mix in the vanilla extract and banana puree.
4. Pour the ingredients into your ice cream maker, and let it churn for 25 minutes. About 5 minutes before the ice cream is done churning add the walnuts to your ice cream maker.
5. Put the gelato in an airtight container and place in the freezer for up to 2 hours, until desired consistency is reached.

Kickin' Key Lime Sorbet

Servings: 4
Cooking Time: 3 Hours

Ingredients:

- 3 cups cold water
- 2 ¼ cup fresh key lime juice
- 2 3/4 cup sugar
- 1 tablespoon lime zest

Directions:

1. Refer to note at the beginning of the chapter about freezing bowl.
2. Mix together the water and sugar in a large sauce pan on medium heat. Allow the mixture to come to a boil. Then lower to low heat, and let the mixture simmer until the sugar dissolve. Allow the mixture to cool completely.
3. Mix the lime juice and zest with the cooled mixture.
4. Pour the ingredients into your ice cream maker, and let it churn for 25-30 minutes.
5. Place in an airtight container for up to 2 hours, until desired consistency is reached.

Big Blueberry Chocolate Gelato

Servings: 4-6
Cooking Time: 2 Hours 35 Minutes

Ingredients:

- 1/2 cup heavy cream
- 2 cups milk
- 3/4 cup sugar
- 1 teaspoon vanilla extract
- 1 cup blueberries
- ½ cup finely chopped semi-sweet

Directions:

1. Refer to note at the beginning of the chapter about freezing bowl.
2. Puree the bananas in a food processor or blender.
3. Place the milk and cream in a bowl, and mix them together until well combined. Use a whisk to mix in the sugar. Continue to whisk for about 4 minutes until the sugar dissolves. Then mix in the vanilla extract and banana puree.
4. Pour the ingredients into your ice cream maker, and let it churn for 25 minutes. About 5 minutes before the ice cream is done churning add the chocolate to your ice cream maker.
5. Put the gelato in an airtight container and place in the freezer for up to 2 hours, until desired consistency is reached.

Pulsating Pomegranate Mint Frozen Yogurt

Servings: 1 Quart
Cooking Time: 2 Hours 35 Minutes

Ingredients:

- 1 quart container full-fat plain yogurt
- ¼ teaspoon salt
- 1 cup sugar
- 1 tablespoon mint extract
- 1 cup 100% pomegranate juice
- 1/2 cup semi-sweet chocolate chips

Directions:

1. Refer to note at the beginning of the chapter about freezing bowl.
2. Place the yogurt in a bowl. Use a whisk to mix in the sugar and salt. Continue to whisk for about 4 minutes until the sugar dissolves. Then mix in the mint extract, and pomegranate juice.
3. Pour the ingredients into your ice cream maker, and let it churn for 25 minutes. About 5 minutes before the ice cream is done churning add the chocolate chips to your ice cream maker.
4. Put the frozen yogurt in an airtight container and place in the freezer for at least 2 hours, until desired consistency is reached.

Astounding Apricot Almond Ice Cream

Servings: 6
Cooking Time: 2 Hours 50 Minutes

Ingredients:

- 2 cups heavy cream
- 1 cup milk
- 3/4 cup sugar
- 1 teaspoon vanilla extract
- 1 cup sliced apricots
- ½ cup chopped almonds

Directions:

1. Refer to note at the beginning of the chapter about freezing bowl.
2. Puree the apricots in a food processor or blender.
3. Place the milk and cream in a bowl, and mix them together until well combined. Use a whisk to mix in the sugar. Continue to whisk for about 4 minutes until the sugar dissolves. Then mix in the vanilla extract, and apricot puree.
4. Pour the ingredients into your ice cream maker, and let it churn for 25 minutes. About 5 minutes before the ice cream is finished churning, add in the almonds.
5. Put the ice cream in an airtight container and place in the freezer for around 2 hours. Allow the ice cream to thaw for 15 minutes before serving.

Chocolate Peppermint Banana Vegan Milkshake

Servings: 9
Cooking Time: 10 Minutes

Ingredients:

- 3/4 cup water
- 1 1/4 cups full fat coconut milk or coconut cream (as thick as possible)
- 2/3 cup organic cane sugar
- 2/3 cup unsweetened cocoa powder
- 1/4 tsp sea salt
- 6 ounces vegan dark chocolate, finely chopped
- 11/2 tsp peppermint extract
- ½ cup sliced frozen bananas

Directions:

1. NOTE: Freeze your ice cream bowl for at least 24hrs prior to starting!
2. Put the first 5 ingredients in a large saucepan, and heat it on medium-high heat. Mix the ingredients together using a whisk. Allow the mixture to come to a low boil. Continue to whisk often, and remain cooking on a low boil for 1 minute.
3. Take the pan off the heat, and mix in the chocolate and mint extract using the whisk. Continue to mix until the chocolate is melted.
4. Place mixture in a blender with the bananas, and blend on high speed for about 30 seconds.
5. Allow the mixture to cool
6. Pour the ingredients into your ice cream maker, and let it churn for 10-15 minutes, until desired consistency is reached.
7. Serve immediately.

Raspberry Pumpkin Spice Vegan Soy Frozen Yogurt

Servings: 1 Quart

Cooking Time: 2 Hours 30 Minutes

Ingredients:

- 2 ¾ cups unsweetened plain soy yogurt
- 1¼ raspberry jam
- 1 tbsp. pumpkin spice

Directions:

1. NOTE: Freeze your ice cream bowl for at least 24hrs prior to starting!
2. Place the yogurt in a bowl and mix in the jam. Use a hand mixer to beat the mixture for 5 minutes.
3. Pour the ingredients into your ice cream maker, and let it churn for 25 minutes.
4. Put the frozen yogurt in an airtight container and place in the freezer for at least 2 hours, until desired consistency is reached.

Peanut Butter White Chocolate Soft Serve Ice Cream

Servings: 6
Cooking Time: 40 Minutes

Ingredients:

- 2 cups heavy cream
- 1 cup milk
- 3⁄4 cup sugar
- 1 Tbs. vanilla extract
- 1/2 cup peanut butter slightly melted
- 2 ounces semi-sweet chocolate

Directions:

1. NOTE: Freeze your ice cream bowl for at least 24hrs prior to starting!
2. Melt the chocolate in a medium sauce pan on low heat. Allow the chocolate to cool a bit.
3. While the chocolate is cooling, place the milk and cream in a bowl, and mix them together until well combined. Use a whisk to mix in the sugar. Continue to whisk for about 4 minutes until the sugar dissolves. Mix in the vanilla extract. Then whisk in the peanut butter, and then the chocolate.
4. Pour the ingredients into your ice cream maker, and let it churn for 25 minutes.
5. Serve immediately.

Lemon Chocolate Blueberry Vegan Gelato

Servings: Makes 3 Cups
Cooking Time: 2 Hours 35 Minutes

Ingredients:

- 1 ½ cup refrigerated coconut cream
- 1 cup cut up lemons
- 3 tablespoons cocoa powder
- 1/2 teaspoon salt
- ½ cup blueberries

Directions:

1. NOTE: Freeze your ice cream bowl for at least 24hrs prior to starting!
2. Place all ingredients EXCEPT the blueberries in a blender. Blend on high speed until smooth.
3. Pour the mixture into your ice cream maker, and let it churn for 25 minutes. About 5 minutes before the ice cream is done churning add the blueberries to your ice cream maker.
4. Put the gelato in an airtight container and place in the freezer for up to 2 hours, until desired consistency is reached.

Rosemary Soft Serve Ice Cream

Servings: 6
Cooking Time: 35 Minutes

Ingredients:

- 2 cups heavy cream
- 1 cup milk
- 3⁄4 cup sugar
- 1 Tbs. vanilla extract
- 1 ½ cups packed rosemary

Directions:

1. NOTE: Freeze your ice cream bowl for at least 24hrs prior to starting!
2. Place the milk and cream in a bowl, and mix them together until well combined. Use a whisk to mix in the sugar. Continue to whisk for about 4 minutes until the sugar dissolves. Mix in the vanilla extract.
3. Pulverize the rosemary in a blender or food processer.
4. Place all the ingredients in a food processor or blender, and puree.
5. Pour the ingredients into your ice cream maker, and let it churn for 25 minutes.
6. Serve immediately.

Kickin' Kiwi Lime Ice Cream

Servings: 6
Cooking Time: 2 Hours 50 Minutes

Ingredients:

- 2 cups heavy cream
- 1 cup milk
- 3/4 cup sugar
- 1/2 teaspoon vanilla extract
- ½ teaspoon salt
- 1 kiwi, peeled
- Juice of one and a half limes

Directions:

1. Refer to note at the beginning of the chapter about freezing bowl.
2. Puree the kiwi in a food processor or blender.
3. Place the milk and cream in a bowl, and mix them together until well combined. Use a whisk to mix in the sugar and salt. Continue to whisk for about 4 minutes until the sugar and salt dissolves. Then mix in the vanilla extract, lime juice, and kiwi puree.
4. Pour the ingredients into your ice cream maker, and let it churn for 25 minutes.
5. Put the ice cream in an airtight container and place in the freezer for around 2 hours. Allow the ice cream to thaw for 15 minutes before serving.

Carob Chip Mint Soy Vanilla Vegan Ice Cream

Servings: Makes 1 Quart
Cooking Time: 35 Minutes

Ingredients:

- 1 pound silken tofu
- ½ cup plus 2 tablespoons organic or granulated sugar
- ½ teaspoon kosher salt
- 1 vanilla bean, split lengthwise
- ¾ cup virgin coconut oil, melted, ½ cooled
- 1 cup vegan carob chips
- ¼ cup mint (pulverized)

Directions:

1. NOTE: Freeze your ice cream bowl for at least 24hrs prior to starting!
2. Put the first 3 ingredients in a blender. Then add in the vanilla bean seeds. Puree the mixture until its smooth, around 15 seconds. Turn the blender to medium speed, and slowly drizzle in the coconut oil. Blend the mixture until its thick, but don't over blend it.
3. Pour the ingredients into your ice cream maker, and let it churn for 25 minutes. About 5 minutes before the ice cream is done churning add the carob chips and mint to your ice cream maker.
4. Put the ice cream in an airtight container and place in the freezer for around 2 hours. Allow the ice cream to thaw for 15 minutes before serving.

Blackberry Lemon Coconut Vegan Frozen Yogurt

Servings: 1 Quart
Cooking Time: 2 Hours 35 Minutes

Ingredients:

- 2 cups coconut yogurt
- 1/4 cup sugar or maple syrup
- 1/2 teaspoon vanilla extract
- 1/4 cup shredded coconut
- ½ cup blackberries
- 1 lemon

Directions:

1. NOTE: Freeze your ice cream bowl for at least 24hrs prior to starting!
2. Puree the blackberries and lemon in a food processor or blender.
3. Place the yogurt in a bowl. Use a whisk to mix in the sugar. Continue to whisk for about 4 minutes until the sugar dissolves. Then mix in the vanilla extract, and blackberry puree.
4. Pour the ingredients into your ice cream maker, and let it churn for 25 minutes. About 5 minutes before the ice cream is done churning add the shredded coconut to your ice cream maker.
5. Put the frozen yogurt in an airtight container and place in the freezer for at least 2 hours, until desired consistency is reached.

VANILLA ICE CREAM

Key Lime Ice Cream Recipe

Servings:x
Cooking Time: X

Ingredients:

- 2 eggs large egg
- 1 <small>1/4</small> cups sugar white sugar
- 4 eggs large egg yolks egg yolks
- 1 tablespoon lemon zest lemon zest
- 2 <small>1/4</small> cups cream half-and-half cream
- 3/4 cup lime juice lime juice

Directions:

1. hisk together the eggs, egg yolks, sugar, lime juice, and lemon zest in a saucepan over medium heat until well-blended. Continuously stir the egg mixture with a wooden spoon until thickened, 7 to 8 minutes. The mixture ought to be thick enough to coat the trunk of the spoon. Remove from heat, and stir in the half and half until smooth. Strain the mixture through a fine sieve set over a clean bowl. Cover and chill the mixture in the refrigerator, stirring occasionally, until cool, about 1 hour.
2. Pour the chilled mixture into an ice cream maker and freeze according to manufacturer's directions until it reaches "soft-serve" consistency. Transfer ice cream to a one- or two-quart lidded plastic container; cover surface with plastic wrap and seal. For best results, ice cream should ripen in the freezer for at least 2 hours or overnight.

Nesquik Frostee No-churn Ice Cream

Servings:x
Cooking Time: X

Ingredients:

- 3 cups heavy cream
- 1 145 cans 1 14.5-oz. sweetened condensed milk
- 1/3 cup Nesquik chocolate flavor powder

Directions:

1. In a big mixing bowl, beat heavy cream using an electric mixer until stiff peaks form, 5 to 6 minutes.
2. Mix in the sweetened condensed milk and Nesquik. Pour mixture right into a loaf pan and freeze for at least 4 hours, or until firm. (The texture is a lot like soft serve.) Optional: Dust ice cream with a light sprinkling of Nesquik powder before serving.

Keto No-churn Strawberry Ice Cream Recipe

Servings:x
Cooking Time: X

Ingredients:

- 1 cup heavy whipping cream
- 1/3 cup chopped strawberries
- 2 tablespoons low-calorie natural sweetener (such as swerve)
- 1 tablespoon vodka
- 1 teaspoon vanilla extract
- 1/4 teaspoon xanthan gum
- 1 pinch salt

Directions:

1. Combine heavy cream, strawberries, sweetener, vodka, vanilla extract, xanthan gum, and salt in a wide-mouth pint-size jar.
2. Using an immersion blender and an along motion, blend cream mixture for 60 to 75 seconds, or until thickened and soft peaks have formed.
3. Cover jar and freeze, stirring every 30 to 40 minutes, until ice cream reaches your ideal consistency, 3 to4 hours.

Easy Ice Cream In A Bag Recipe

Servings:x
Cooking Time: X

Ingredients:

- 1/4 cup milk
- 1/4 cup half-and-half
- 1 tablespoon white sugar
- 1/4 teaspoon vanilla extract
- 1 cup ice cubes, or as needed
- 3 tablespoons ice cream rock salt

Directions:

1. Combine milk, half-and-half, sugar, and vanilla extract in a pint-size resealable plastic bag; seal tightly.
2. Put a scoop of ice, 3 tablespoons ice cream rock salt, and the bag containing the milk-cream mixture right into a gallon-size resealable plastic bag; seal tightly.
3. Rock the bag backwards and forwards (usually do not shake) until contents thicken into ice cream, about 10 minutes. Wipe salt from the very best of the pint-size bag before opening to prevent salt from getting into the ice cream.

Tropical Avocado Ice Cream

Servings:x
Cooking Time: X

Ingredients:

- 4 avocados , peeled and pitted
- 1 cup lime juice (about 4 juicy limes)
- zest of 2 lime
- 1 cup maple syrup
- 2 cans coconut cream
- 2 teaspoons vanilla extract
- 2 tablespoons coconut oils
- 1/2 teaspoon kosher salt
- 1/2 lime, thinly sliced into quarters, for garnish

Directions:

1. Combine all ingredients, except lime slices, in a blender. Blend on high until smooth.
2. Pour into loaf pan and garnish with lime slices. Freeze until firm, at least 3 hours or overnight.

Vanilla Ice Cream V Recipe

Servings:x
Cooking Time: X

Ingredients:

- 2 quarts half-and-half cream
- 1/2 pint heavy cream
- 1 1/2 cups white sugar
- 4 teaspoons vanilla extract
- 1 pinch salt

Directions:

1. Combine half-and-half, cream, sugar, vanilla and salt in freezer container of ice cream maker.
2. Freeze according to manufacturer's instructions.

Peanut Butter-banana V'ice Cream

Servings:x
Cooking Time: X

Ingredients:

- 4 very ripe bananas
- 1/4 cup peanut butter (smooth or chunky)
- 1 tablespoon coconut oils
- 1/2 teaspoon ground cinnamon
- 1/4 teaspoon grated nutmeg
- pinch of kosher salt

Directions:

1. Slice bananas into 1/4”-thick rounds and devote a ziptop plastic bag. Lay the slices flat in a single layer in the freezer therefore the rounds freeze individually rather than in a large clump.
2. Freeze the bananas for at least 2 hours and up to overnight. Place the frozen bananas, peanut butter, coconut oil, cinnamon, nutmeg, and salt in a food processor or blender and let sit for 2 or 3 three minutes. Then puree until creamy and smooth. If you like a frozen yogurt consistency, then serve it up.
3. If you like a firmer ice cream experience, spoon it right into a container and freeze for approximately an hour.

Peach-maple Ice Cream

Servings:x
Cooking Time: X

Ingredients:

- 3/4 pound ripe peaches
- 1 tablespoon fresh lemon juice
- 1 cup heavy cream
- 1/2 cup milk
- 1/2 vanilla bean , split, seeds scraped
- 2 large eggs yolks
- 1/4 cup plus 2 tablespoons sugar
- pinch of salt
- 1/4 cup pure maple syrup
- 1 tablespoon bourbon, or more to taste

Directions:

1. Bring a little pot of water to a boil and fill a medium bowl with ice water. Cut a shallow X in the bottom of every peach and plunge it into the boiling water for 30 seconds. Transfer the peaches to the ice water to cool. Peel the peaches and cut them into 1/2-inch wedges; reserve the peach skins and pits. Transfer the peaches to a bowl and toss with the lemon juice. Cover the peaches and refrigerate.
2. In a medium saucepan, combine the cream and milk. Add the vanilla bean and seeds and peach skins and pits and bring to a simmer. Cover and remove from the heat. Let steep for 20 minutes. Strain the infused cream right into a bowl.
3. In a medium bowl, whisk the egg yolks with the sugar and salt. Whisk in half of the infused cream, then transfer the mixture to the saucepan, together with the remaining cream. Cook over moderate heat, stirring constantly with a wooden spoon, until slightly thickened and an instant-read thermometer inserted in the custard registers 165°, about five minutes. Immediately strain the custard into a clean bowl and stir in the maple syrup and bourbon. Refrigerate the custard until chilled, about 30 minutes.
4. In a blender, puree the peaches with 1 cup of the custard until smooth. Transfer the pureed peaches and the remaining custard to an ice cream maker and freeze according to the manufacturer's instructions. Transfer the ice cream to a plastic container. Press a sheet of plastic wrap directly onto the top and freeze until firm, about one hour.

Frozen Strawberry Yogurt Recipe

Servings:x
Cooking Time: X

Ingredients:

- 1 pound fresh strawberries
- 3/4 cup white sugar
- 1 tablespoon vanilla extract
- 1/4 cup half-and-half
- 1 (32-ounce) container plain yogurt

Directions:

1. Place strawberries, sugar, vanilla extract, and half-and-half in a blender; puree until smooth. Add yogurt and pulse until combined.
2. Pour the mixture into an ice cream maker and freeze according to manufacturer's instructions. Transfer frozen yogurt to a lidded plastic container. Cover surface with plastic wrap and seal. For best results, let it ripen in the freezer for at least 2 hours or overnight before serving.

Lavender Honey Ice Cream Recipe

Servings:x
Cooking Time: X

Ingredients:

- 2 cups heavy whipping cream
- 1 cup half-and-half
- 2/3 cup honey
- 2 tablespoons dried lavender flowers
- 2 large eggs
- teaspoon ? salt

Directions:

1. Heat heavy cream, half-and-half, honey, and lavender flowers in a heavy 2-quart saucepan, stirring occasionally, until cream just starts to bubble. Remove from heat and cover; let steep for thirty minutes.
2. Strain cream mixture right into a bowl utilizing a fine-mesh sieve. Discard lavender flowers. Clean saucepan and pour strained cream mixture back in. Heat over medium heat until hot, about five minutes.
3. Whisk eggs and salt together in a bowl. Whisk in 1 cup hot cream in a slow stream.
4. Pour egg mixture in to the remaining hot cream in the saucepan. Cook over medium-low heat, stirring constantly with a wooden spoon, until custard coats the trunk of the spoon and reads 175 degrees F (80 degrees C) on an instant-read thermometer, about five minutes.
5. Pour custard through a fine-mesh sieve into a bowl. Let cool completely, stirring occasionally, about a quarter-hour. Chill, covered, for at least 3 hours.
6. Freeze custard in an ice cream maker according to manufacturer's instructions, about 20 minutes. Transfer to an airtight container and place in the freezer to set.

Spiced Ginger-peach Ice Cream Recipe

Servings:x
Cooking Time: X

Ingredients:

- 1 cup milk
- 3/4 cup white sugar
- 1/4 teaspoon salt
- 3 ounces peach puree
- 3/4 teaspoon ground ginger
- 1/2 teaspoon ground cinnamon , or more to taste
- 1/4 teaspoon vanilla extract
- 3 large eggs yolks egg yolks, lightly beaten
- 2 cups heavy whipping cream
- 4 small slice (blank)s fresh peach slices, diced, or more to taste

Directions:

1. Whisk milk, sugar, and salt together in a saucepan over medium heat; bring to a simmer. Stir peach puree, ginger, cinnamon, and vanilla extract; simmer until flavors blend, 5 to 10 minutes.
2. Place egg yolks in a little bowl. Slowly pour 1/2 cup hot milk mixture into eggs, whisking constantly. Pour warmed egg mixture into the milk mixture in the saucepan over medium heat. Cook, stirring occasionally, until thick, 5 to ten minutes. Strain egg mixture right into a chilled bowl and refrigerate, stirring occasionally, until chilled, about 2 hours.
3. Whisk cream into chilled egg mixture; add peaches and stir.
4. Pour peach mixture in to the container of an ice cream maker and freeze according to the manufacturer's instructions.

Strawberry Rosewater Ice Cream Recipe

Servings:x
Cooking Time: X

Ingredients:

- 1 1/2 cups fresh strawberries , hulled
- 1/3 cup white sugar
- 3 eaches eggs yolks, beaten
- 1/2 pint milk
- 1/4 teaspoon salt
- 1/3 cup white sugar
- 1 pint heavy cream
- 1/4 cup rosewater

Directions:

1. Combine the strawberries and 1/3 cup sugar in a bowl; mash as well as a potato masher. Store the mixture in the refrigerator while preparing all of those other recipe.
2. Stir together the egg yolks, milk, salt and 1/3 cup sugar in a saucepan over medium heat. Heat to 175 degrees F (80 degrees C), making sure the mixture will not boil; transfer to a chilled bowl and move to the refrigerator to cool, stirring occasionally. Once cooled, stir in the cream, rosewater, and strawberry mixture.
3. Fill an ice cream maker with the mixture, and freeze based on the manufacturer's instructions.

French-style Ice Cream

Servings:x
Cooking Time: X

Ingredients:

- 6 eggs large egg yolks
- 3/4 cup sugar
- 1 <small>3/4</small> cups heavy cream heavy cream
- 1 <small>1/4</small> cups milk whole milk
- pinch salt of salt

Directions:

1. Set a medium bowl in a sizable bowl of ice water. In another medium bowl, whisk the egg yolks with 1/2 cup of the sugar until pale, about three minutes.
2. In a medium saucepan, combine the cream, milk, salt and remaining 1/4 cup of sugar and bring to a simmer, whisking before sugar is completely dissolved. Whisk the hot cream mixture in to the beaten egg yolks in a thin stream.
3. Transfer the mixture to the saucepan and cook over moderately low heat, stirring constantly with a wooden spoon, before custard is thick enough to lightly coat the trunk of the spoon, about 4 minutes; don't let it boil. Pour the custard through a fine-mesh strainer in to the medium bowl in the ice water. Let cool completely, stirring frequently. Refrigerate the custard until cold, at least one hour.
4. Pour the custard into an ice cream maker with flavorings, if using, and freeze based on the manufacturer's instructions. Transfer the frozen custard to a plastic container, cover and freeze until firm, at least 3 hours

CANDY BAR FUSION ICE CREAM

Mars Bar Soft Serve Ice Cream

Servings: 6
Cooking Time: 35 Minutes

Ingredients:

- 2 cups heavy cream
- 1 cup milk
- 3⁄4 cup sugar
- 1 Tbs. vanilla extract
- 1 cup sliced Bananas
- 2 Mars Bar Candy Bars.

Directions:

1. Refer to note at the beginning of the chapter about freezing bowl.
2. Place the milk & cream in a bowl. Mix together until well combined. Use a whisk to mix in the sugar. Continue to whisking 4 minutes until sugar dissolves. Then mix in the vanilla extract.
3. Place all the ingredients in a food processor or blender, and puree.
4. Pour ingredients into ice cream maker. Let it churn for 25 minutes.

3 Musketeers Soft Serve Ice Cream

Servings: 6
Cooking Time: 35 Minutes

Ingredients:

- 2 cups heavy cream
- 1 cup milk
- 3⁄4 cup sugar
- 1 Tbs. vanilla extract
- 1 cup sliced Bananas
- 2 3 Musketeers Candy Bars.

Directions:

1. Refer to note at the beginning of the chapter about freezing bowl.
2. Place the milk & cream in a bowl. Mix together until well combined. Use a whisk to mix in the sugar. Continue to whisking 4 minutes until sugar dissolves. Then mix in the vanilla extract.
3. Place all the ingredients in a food processor or blender, and puree.
4. Pour ingredients into ice cream maker. Let it churn for 25 minutes.

5th Avenue Soft Serve Ice Cream

Servings: 6
Cooking Time: 35 Minutes

Ingredients:

- 2 cups heavy cream
- 1 cup milk
- 3⁄4 cup sugar
- 1 Tbs. vanilla extract
- 1 cup sliced Bananas
- 2 5th Avenue Candy Bars.

Directions:

1. Refer to note at the beginning of the chapter about freezing bowl.
2. Place the milk & cream in a bowl. Mix together until well combined. Use a whisk to mix in the sugar. Continue to whisking 4 minutes until sugar dissolves. Then mix in the vanilla extract.
3. Place all the ingredients in a food processor or blender, and puree.
4. Pour ingredients into ice cream maker. Let it churn for 25 minutes.
5. Serve immediately.

Whatchamacallit Soft Serve Ice Cream

Servings: 6
Cooking Time: 35 Minutes

Ingredients:

- 2 cups heavy cream
- 1 cup milk
- 3⁄4 cup sugar
- 1 Tbs. vanilla extract
- 1 cup sliced Bananas
- 2 Whatchamacallit Candy Bars.

Directions:

1. Refer to note at the beginning of the chapter about freezing bowl.
2. Place the milk & cream in a bowl. Mix together until well combined. Use a whisk to mix in the sugar. Continue to whisking 4 minutes until sugar dissolves. Then mix in the vanilla extract.
3. Place all the ingredients in a food processor or blender, and puree.
4. Pour ingredients into ice cream maker. Let it churn for 25 minutes.

Butterfinger Soft Serve Ice Cream

Servings: 6
Cooking Time: 35 Minutes

Ingredients:

- 2 cups heavy cream
- 1 cup milk
- 3⁄4 cup sugar
- 1 Tbs. vanilla extract
- 1 cup sliced Bananas
- 2 Butterfinger Candy Bars.

Directions:

1. Refer to note at the beginning of the chapter about freezing bowl.
2. Place the milk & cream in a bowl. Mix together until well combined. Use a whisk to mix in the sugar. Continue to whisking 4 minutes until sugar dissolves. Then mix in the vanilla extract.
3. Place all the ingredients in a food processor or blender, and puree.
4. Pour ingredients into ice cream maker. Let it churn for 25 minutes.
5. Serve immediately.

Caramello Dreamin Soft Serve Ice Cream

Servings: 6
Cooking Time: 35 Minutes

Ingredients:

- 2 cups heavy cream
- 1 cup milk
- 3⁄4 cup sugar
- 1 Tbs. vanilla extract
- 1 cup sliced Bananas
- 2 Caramello Candy Bars.

Directions:

1. Refer to note at the beginning of the chapter about freezing bowl.
2. Place the milk & cream in a bowl. Mix together until well combined. Use a whisk to mix in the sugar. Continue to whisking 4 minutes until sugar dissolves. Then mix in the vanilla extract.
3. Place all the ingredients in a food processor or blender, and puree.
4. Pour ingredients into ice cream maker. Let it churn for 25 minutes.
5. Serve immediately.

Skor Bar Soft Serve Ice Cream

Servings: 6
Cooking Time: 35 Minutes

Ingredients:

- 2 cups heavy cream
- 1 cup milk
- 3⁄4 cup sugar
- 1 Tbs. vanilla extract
- 1 cup sliced Bananas
- 2 Skor Bar Candy Bars.

Directions:

1. Refer to note at the beginning of the chapter about freezing bowl.
2. Place the milk & cream in a bowl. Mix together until well combined. Use a whisk to mix in the sugar. Continue to whisking 4 minutes until sugar dissolves. Then mix in the vanilla extract.
3. Place all the ingredients in a food processor or blender, and puree.
4. Pour ingredients into ice cream maker. Let it churn for 25 minutes.
5. Serve immediately.

Hershey Bar Soft Serve Ice Cream

Servings: 6
Cooking Time: 35 Minutes

Ingredients:

- 2 cups heavy cream
- 1 cup milk
- 3⁄4 cup sugar
- 1 Tbs. vanilla extract
- 1 cup sliced Bananas
- 2 Hershey Bar Candy Bars.

Directions:

1. Refer to note at the beginning of the chapter about freezing bowl.
2. Place the milk & cream in a bowl. Mix together until well combined. Use a whisk to mix in the sugar. Continue to whisking 4 minutes until sugar dissolves. Then mix in the vanilla extract.
3. Place all the ingredients in a food processor or blender, and puree.
4. Pour ingredients into ice cream maker. Let it churn for 25 minutes.
5. Serve immediately.

Mounds Soft Serve Ice Cream

Servings: 6
Cooking Time: 35 Minutes

Ingredients:

- 2 cups heavy cream
- 1 cup milk
- 3⁄4 cup sugar
- 1 Tbs. vanilla extract
- 1 cup sliced Bananas
- 2 Mounds Candy Bars.

Directions:

1. Refer to note at the beginning of the chapter about freezing bowl.
2. Place the milk & cream in a bowl. Mix together until well combined. Use a whisk to mix in the sugar. Continue to whisking 4 minutes until sugar dissolves. Then mix in the vanilla extract.
3. Place all the ingredients in a food processor or blender, and puree.
4. Pour ingredients into ice cream maker. Let it churn for 25 minutes.

Krackel Soft Serve Ice Cream

Servings: 6
Cooking Time: 35 Minutes

Ingredients:

- 2 cups heavy cream
- 1 cup milk
- 3⁄4 cup sugar
- 1 Tbs. vanilla extract
- 1 cup sliced Bananas
- 2 Krackel Candy Bars.

Directions:

1. Refer to note at the beginning of the chapter about freezing bowl.
2. Place the milk & cream in a bowl. Mix together until well combined. Use a whisk to mix in the sugar. Continue to whisking 4 minutes until sugar dissolves. Then mix in the vanilla extract.
3. Place all the ingredients in a food processor or blender, and puree.
4. Pour ingredients into ice cream maker. Let it churn for 25 minutes.

Snickers Soft Serve Ice Cream

Servings: 6
Cooking Time: 35 Minutes

Ingredients:

- 2 cups heavy cream
- 1 cup milk
- 3⁄4 cup sugar
- 1 Tbs. vanilla extract
- 1 cup sliced Bananas
- 2 Snickers Candy Bars.

Directions:

1. Refer to note at the beginning of the chapter about freezing bowl.
2. Place the milk & cream in a bowl. Mix together until well combined. Use a whisk to mix in the sugar. Continue to whisking 4 minutes until sugar dissolves. Then mix in the vanilla extract.
3. Place all the ingredients in a food processor or blender, and puree.
4. Pour ingredients into ice cream maker. Let it churn for 25 minutes.

Charleston Chew Soft Serve Ice Cream

Servings: 6
Cooking Time: 35 Minutes

Ingredients:

- 2 cups heavy cream
- 1 cup milk
- 3⁄4 cup sugar
- 1 Tbs. vanilla extract
- 1 cup sliced Bananas
- 2 Charleston Chew Candy Bars.

Directions:

1. Refer to note at the beginning of the chapter about freezing bowl.
2. Place the milk & cream in a bowl. Mix together until well combined. Use a whisk to mix in the sugar. Continue to whisking 4 minutes until sugar dissolves. Then mix in the vanilla extract.
3. Place all the ingredients in a food processor or blender, and puree.
4. Pour ingredients into ice cream maker. Let it churn for 25 minutes.

Kit Kat Soft Serve Ice Cream

Servings: 6
Cooking Time: 35 Minutes

Ingredients:

- 2 cups heavy cream
- 1 cup milk
- 3⁄4 cup sugar
- 1 Tbs. vanilla extract
- 1 cup sliced Bananas
- 2 Kit Kat Candy Bars.

Directions:

1. Refer to note at the beginning of the chapter about freezing bowl.
2. Place the milk & cream in a bowl. Mix together until well combined. Use a whisk to mix in the sugar. Continue to whisking 4 minutes until sugar dissolves. Then mix in the vanilla extract.
3. Place all the ingredients in a food processor or blender, and puree.
4. Pour ingredients into ice cream maker. Let it churn for 25 minutes.

THE CLASSICS ICE CREAM

The Original "manhattan" Ice Cream

Servings: 6
Cooking Time: 2 Hours 50 Minutes

Ingredients:

- 2 cups heavy cream
- 1 cup milk
- 3/4 cup sugar
- 1 tablespoon vanilla extract
- 3 tablespoons whiskey
- 1 tablespoon vermouth
- 1 dash of bitters

Directions:

1. NOTE: Freeze your ice cream bowl for at least 24hrs prior to starting!
2. Place the milk and cream in a bowl, and mix them together until well combined. Use a whisk to mix in the sugar. Continue to whisk for about 4 minutes until the sugar dissolves. Then mix in the vanilla extract, whiskey, vermouth, and bitters.
3. Pour the ingredients into your ice cream maker, and let it churn for 25 minutes.
4. Put the ice cream in an airtight container and place in the freezer for around 2 hours. Allow the ice cream to thaw for 15 minutes before serving.

Margarita Madness Soft Serve Ice Cream

Servings: 6
Cooking Time: 35 Minutes

Ingredients:

- 2 cups heavy cream
- 1 cup milk
- 3⁄4 cup sugar
- 1 Tbs. vanilla extract
- 3 tablespoons tequila
- 1/2 cup lime juice
- 2 tablespoons orange liqueur

Directions:

1. Refer to note at the beginning of the chapter about freezing bowl.
2. Place the milk and cream in a bowl, and mix them together until well combined. Use a whisk to mix in the sugar. Continue to whisk for about 4 minutes until the sugar dissolves. Mix in the vanilla extract. Finally whisk in the lime juice, tequila, and liqueur.
3. Pour the ingredients into your ice cream maker, and let it churn for 25 minutes.
4. Serve immediately.

Sunrise Strawberry Daiquiri Milkshake

Servings: 6
Cooking Time: 25 Minutes

Ingredients:

- 2 cups heavy cream
- 1 cup milk
- 3/4 cup sugar
- 4 tablespoons rum
- 8 ounces strawberries

Directions:

1. Refer to note at the beginning of the chapter about freezing bowl.
2. Puree the strawberries in a food processor or blender.
3. Place the milk and cream in a bowl, and mix them together until well combined. Use a whisk to mix in the sugar. Continue to whisk for about 4 minutes until the sugar dissolves. Then mix in the rum, and strawberry puree.
4. Pour the ingredients into your ice cream maker, and let it churn for 10-15 minutes, until desired consistency is reached. About 5 minutes before the ice cream is done churning add the peanut butter cup to your ice cream maker.
5. Serve immediately.

California Cookies-n-cream Soft Serve Ice Cream

Servings: 6
Cooking Time: 35 Minutes

Ingredients:

- 2 cups heavy cream
- 1 cup milk
- 3⁄4 cup sugar
- 1 Tbs. vanilla extract
- 20 chocolate sandwich cookies

Directions:

1. Refer to note at the beginning of the chapter about freezing bowl.
2. Place the milk and cream in a bowl, and mix them together until well combined. Use a whisk to mix in the sugar. Continue to whisk for about 4 minutes until the sugar dissolves. Then mix in the vanilla extract.
3. Place the sandwich cookies in a food processor, and process until the cookies are no bigger than chocolate chips. If you don't have a food processor place the cookies in a large resealable plastic bag, and seal it shut. Use your hands, a mallet, or a rolling pin to crush the cookies.
4. Pour the ingredients into your ice cream maker, and let it churn for 25 minutes. About 5 minutes before the ice cream is finished churning, add in the chocolate sandwich cookies.
5. Serve immediately.

Miraculous Double Mint Chip Ice Cream

Servings: 6
Cooking Time: 2 Hours 50 Minutes

Ingredients:

- 2 cups heavy cream
- 1 cup milk
- 3/4 cup sugar
- 1 teaspoon vanilla extract
- 1 teaspoon peppermint extract
- 1 cup semi-sweet chocolate chips

Directions:

1. Refer to note at the beginning of the chapter about freezing bowl.
2. Place the milk and cream in a bowl, and mix them together until well combined. Use a whisk to mix in the sugar. Continue to whisk for about 4 minutes until the sugar dissolves. Then mix in the vanilla and peppermint extract.
3. Pour the ingredients into your ice cream maker, and let it churn for 25 minutes. About 5 minutes before the ice cream is finished churning, add in the chocolate chips.
4. Put the ice cream in an airtight container and place in the freezer for around 2 hours. Allow the ice cream to thaw for 15 minutes before serving.

Runnin' Rum And Coke Gelato

Servings: 4-6
Cooking Time: 2 Hours 50 Minutes

Ingredients:

- 1/2 cup heavy cream
- 2 cups milk
- 3/4 cup sugar
- 1 teaspoon vanilla extract
- 3 tablespoons rum
- 3 cups coca cola (2, 12 ounce cans)

Directions:

1. Refer to note at the beginning of the chapter about freezing bowl.
2. Pour the coke into a large skillet, and heat it on high heat until it comes to a boil. Allow the coke to cook for about another 15 or 20 minutes, until the coke reduces down to 1 cup of liquid. Let the liquid cool.
3. Place the milk and cream in a bowl, and mix them together until well combined. Use a whisk to mix in the sugar. Continue to whisk for about 4 minutes until the sugar dissolves. Then mix in the vanilla extract, coke reduction, and rum.
4. Pour the ingredients into your ice cream maker, and let it churn for 25 minutes.
5. Put the gelato in an airtight container and place in the freezer for up to 2 hours, until desired consistency is reached.

Creamy Kahlua Almond Delight Ice Cream

Servings: 6
Cooking Time: 2 Hours 50 Minutes

Ingredients:

- 2 cups heavy cream
- 1 cup milk
- 3/4 cup sugar
- 1 teaspoon vanilla extract
- 3 tablespoons kahlua
- 3/4 cup chops almond

Directions:

1. Refer to note at the beginning of the chapter about freezing bowl.
2. Place the milk and cream in a bowl, and mix them together until well combined. Use a whisk to mix in the sugar. Continue to whisk for about 4 minutes until the sugar dissolves. Then mix in the vanilla extract, kahlua.
3. Pour the ingredients into your ice cream maker, and let it churn for 25 minutes. About 5 minutes before the ice cream is done churning add the almonds to your ice cream maker.
4. Put the ice cream in an airtight container and place in the freezer for around 2 hours. Allow the ice cream to thaw for 15 minutes before serving.

Lemon Tequila "sunset" Gelato

Servings: 4-6
Cooking Time: 2 Hours 35 Minutes

Ingredients:

- 1/2 cup heavy cream
- 2 cups milk
- 3/4 cup sugar
- I/2 cup lemon juice
- 1 teaspoon vanilla extract
- 3 tablespoons tequila
- ½ tablespoon grenadine

Directions:

1. NOTE: Freeze your ice cream bowl for at least 24hrs prior to starting!
2. Place the milk and cream in a bowl, and mix them together until well combined. Use a whisk to mix in the sugar. Continue to whisk for about 4 minutes until the sugar dissolves. Then mix in the vanilla extract, lemon juice, tequila and grenadine.
3. Pour the ingredients into your ice cream maker, and let it churn for 25 minutes.
4. Put the gelato in an airtight container and place in the freezer for up to 2 hours, until desired consistency is reached.

Very Strawberry Gelato

Servings: 4-6
Cooking Time: 2 Hours 35 Minutes

Ingredients:

- 1/2 cup heavy cream
- 2 cups milk
- 3/4 cup sugar
- 1 cup sliced strawberries
- 1 tablespoon vanilla extract

Directions:

1. Refer to note at the beginning of the chapter about freezing bowl.
2. Puree the strawberries in a food processor or blender.
3. Place the milk and cream in a bowl, and mix them together until well combined. Use a whisk to mix in the sugar. Continue to whisk for about 4 minutes until the sugar dissolves. Then mix in the vanilla extract and strawberry puree.
4. Pour the ingredients into your ice cream maker, and let it churn for 25 minutes.
5. Put the gelato in an airtight container and place in the freezer for up to 2 hours, until desired consistency is reached.

Mango Strawberry Mint Daiquiri Milkshake

Servings: 6
Cooking Time: 25 Minutes

Ingredients:

- 2 cups heavy cream
- 1 cup milk
- 3/4 cup sugar
- 8 ounces strawberries
- ¼ cup mint
- ¼ cup mango
- 4 tablespoons rum

Directions:

1. NOTE: Freeze your ice cream bowl for at least 24hrs prior to starting!
2. Puree the strawberries, mango and mint in a food processor or blender.
3. Place the milk and cream in a bowl, and mix them together until well combined. Use a whisk to mix in the sugar. Continue to whisk for about 4 minutes until the sugar dissolves. Then mix in the rum, and strawberry puree.
4. Pour the ingredients into your ice cream maker, and let it churn for 10-15 minutes, until desired consistency is reached. About 5 minutes before the ice cream is done churning add the peanut butter cup to your ice cream maker.
5. Serve immediately.

Power Punch Pistachio Ice Cream

Servings: 6
Cooking Time: 2 Hours 50 Minutes

Ingredients:

- 2 cups heavy cream
- 1 cup milk
- 3/4 cup sugar
- 1/4 teaspoon almond extract
- 1/2 cup chopped pistachios

Directions:

1. Refer to note at the beginning of the chapter about freezing bowl.
2. Place the milk and cream in a bowl, and mix them together until well combined. Use a whisk to mix in the sugar. Continue to whisk for about 4 minutes until the sugar dissolves. Then mix in the almond extract.
3. Pour the ingredients into your ice cream maker, and let it churn for 25 minutes. About 5 minutes before the ice cream is finished churning, add in the pistachios.
4. Put the ice cream in an airtight container and place in the freezer for around 2 hours. Allow the ice cream to thaw for 15 minutes before serving.

Mint Cookies 'n Cream "silkshake"

Servings: 6
Cooking Time: 25 Minutes

Ingredients:

- 2 cups heavy cream
- 1 cup milk
- 3/4 cup sugar
- 1 teaspoon vanilla extract
- 1 ½ teaspoons mint extract
- 10 chocolate sandwich cookies

Directions:

1. Refer to note at the beginning of the chapter about freezing bowl.
2. Place the milk and cream in a bowl, and mix them together until well combined. Use a whisk to mix in the sugar. Continue to whisk for about 4 minutes until the sugar dissolves. Then mix in the vanilla and mint extract.
3. Place the sandwich cookies in a food processor, and process until the cookies are no bigger than chocolate chips. If you don't have a food processor place the cookies in a large resealable plastic bag, and seal it shut. Use your hands, a mallet, or a rolling pin to crush the cookies.
4. Pour the ingredients into your ice cream maker, and let it churn for 10-15 minutes, until desired consistency is reached. About 5 minutes before the ice cream is done churning add the cookies to your ice cream maker.
5. Serve immediately.

Pralines And "oh So Creamy" Milkshake

Servings: 6
Cooking Time: 25 Minutes

Ingredients:

- 2 cups heavy cream
- 1 cup milk
- 1 cup brown sugar
- 1 teaspoon vanilla extract
- 1/3 cup finely chopped pecans
- 1 tablespoon butter

Directions:

1. Refer to note at the beginning of the chapter about freezing bowl.
2. Melt the butter in a small skillet on medium heat. Add the pecans, and cook for about 5 minutes, until they become lightly browned.
3. Place the milk and cream in a bowl, and mix them together until well combined. Use a whisk to mix in the sugar. Continue to whisk for about 4 minutes until the sugar dissolves. Then mix in the vanilla extract.
4. Pour the ingredients into your ice cream maker, and let it churn for 10-15 minutes, until desired consistency is reached. About 5 minutes before the ice cream is done churning add the cookie dough to your ice cream maker.
5. Serve immediately.

OTHER FAVORITE RECIPES

Matcha Ice Cream

Servings: 6
Cooking Time: 2 Hours 50 Minutes

Ingredients:

- 2 cups heavy cream
- 1 cup milk
- 3/4 cup sugar
- 1 teaspoon vanilla extract
- 1 tablespoon matcha

Directions:

1. Refer to note at the beginning of the chapter about freezing bowl.
2. Place the milk and cream in a bowl, and mix them together until well combined. Use a whisk to mix in the sugar. Continue to whisk for about 4 minutes until the sugar dissolves. Then mix in the vanilla extract. Finally whisk in the matcha until well mixed.
3. Pour the ingredients into your ice cream maker, and let it churn for 25 minutes.
4. Put the ice cream in an airtight container and place in the freezer for around 2 hours. Allow the ice cream to thaw for 15 minutes before serving.

Plum Sorbet

Servings: Makes 1 Quart
Cooking Time: 4 Hours 35 Minutes

Ingredients:

- 2 pounds pitted, quartered plums
- 1 tablespoon light corn syrup
- 1 cup sugar
- ¼ teaspoon salt

Directions:

1. Refer to note at the beginning of the chapter about freezing bowl.
2. Use a food processor or blender to puree the plums. Put in the sugar and corn syrup, and process for about another 30 seconds. Then blend in the salt. Strain the mixture into a bowl, and refrigerate covered for 2-3 hours.
3. Pour the ingredients into your ice cream maker, and let it churn for 25-30 minutes.
4. Place in an airtight container for up to 2 hours, until desired consistency is reached.

Berries Sorbet

Servings: 8
Cooking Time: 15 Minutes

Ingredients:

- 1/3 cup water
- ¼ cup sugar
- 1 12-ounce package frozen blackberries
- 4 cups mixed berries

Directions:

1. Place water and sugar in a saucepan. Bring to a boil until sugar dissolves. Remove from heat and allow to chill in the fridge for at least 2 hours.
2. Place all ingredients in a blender. Pulse until smooth.
3. Turn on the Cuisinart and pour in the mixture.
4. Churn for 10 minutes.
5. Transfer in an airtight container and freeze overnight.

Nutrition:

- InfoCalories per serving:299 ; Protein: 4.3g; Carbs: 56.5g; Fat: 7.2g Sugar: 20.1g

Berry Ice Cream Cake

Servings: 8
Cooking Time:25 Minutes

Ingredients:

- 1 cup graham crackers, crushed
- ¼ cup butter
- 1 cup cold whole milk
- ¾ cup granulated sugar
- 2 cups cold heavy cream
- 1 teaspoon vanilla extract
- 2 cups of frozen berries, assorted

Directions:

1. In a bowl, mix together the graham crackers and butter to form a dough. Press dough in spring form pan and place in the fridge to chill.
2. Put ice water in a large mixing bowl. Place a small bowl on top of the large bowl with ice. Pour cold milk and sugar into the small bowl and whisk until the sugar is dissolved. Stir in the cream and vanilla. Stir to combine.
3. Place the cold freezer bowl in the Cuisinart Ice Cream Maker. Turn on the machine and pour in the mixture. Add one package of crushed Oreos five minutes before the time ends.
4. Stop in 25 minutes until the mixture becomes soft and creamy.
5. Transfer into a prepared spring form pan and top with berries of your choice.
6. Freeze for 4 hours.
7. Cut into wedges before serving.

Nutrition:

- InfoCalories per serving:277 ; Protein: 2.9g; Carbs: 23.8g; Fat: 19.5g Sugar: 23g

Berry Frozen Yogurt

Servings: 12
Cooking Time: 10 Minutes

Ingredients:

- ¾ cup whole milk
- ¼ cup sugar
- 4 cups Greek yogurt
- 2 cups frozen mixed berries, thawed and pureed

Directions:

1. Place all ingredients in a food processor. Pulse until smooth. Place in the fridge to chill.
2. Turn on the Cuisinart and pour in the mixture.
3. Churn for 10 minutes.
4. Transfer in an airtight container and freeze overnight.

Nutrition:

- InfoCalories per serving: 109; Protein: 4.2g; Carbs: 14.2g; Fat: 4.2g Sugar: 13.6g

Banana Pineapple Coconut Gelato

Servings: 4-6
Cooking Time: 2 Hours 35 Minutes

Ingredients:

- 1/2 cup heavy cream
- 2 cups milk
- 3/4 cup sugar
- 1 tablespoon vanilla extract
- ½ cup sliced banana
- ½ cup chopped pineapple
- ½ cup chopped coconut

Directions:

1. NOTE: Freeze your ice cream bowl for at least 24hrs prior to starting!
2. Puree the bananas in a food processor or blender.
3. Place the milk and cream in a bowl, and mix them together until well combined. Use a whisk to mix in the sugar. Continue to whisk for about 4 minutes until the sugar dissolves. Then mix in the vanilla extract and banana puree.
4. Pour the ingredients into your ice cream maker, and let it churn for 25 minutes. About 5 minutes before the ice cream is done churning add the walnuts to your ice cream maker.
5. Put the gelato in an airtight container and place in the freezer for up to 2 hours, until desired consistency is reached.

"stuffed" Snickers Soft Serve Ice Cream

Servings: 6
Cooking Time: 35 Minutes

Ingredients:

- 2 cups heavy cream
- 1 cup milk
- 3⁄4 cup sugar
- 1 Tbs. vanilla extract
- 1 ½ cups chopped mini snickers bars

Directions:

1. Refer to note at the beginning of the chapter about freezing bowl.
2. Place the milk and cream in a bowl, and mix them together until well combined. Use a whisk to mix in the sugar. Continue to whisk for about 4 minutes until the sugar dissolves. Mix in the vanilla extract.
3. Pour the ingredients into your ice cream maker, and let it churn for 25 minutes. About 5 minutes before the ice cream is done churning add the snickers to your ice cream maker.
4. Serve immediately.

Honey Cinnamon Blackberry English Muffin Ice Cream Sandwich

Servings: 2

Cooking Time: 15 Min

Ingredients:

- 1 pack of English muffins
- organic honey to pour atop
- small pack of blackberries
- 1 tsp. cinnamon

Directions:

1. Toast your English muffins in a toaster just like you would for breakfast.
2. Spread about 4-5 blackberries on top of your warm muffin.
3. Squeeze out and drizzle honey over both inside pieces of the English muffin.
4. Sprinkle a little cinnamon on top
5. Add a scoop of Ice Cream (that you made from this book) between the two pieces of English muffins. Enjoy!

Cinnamon Clove Coffee Frozen Yogurt

Servings: 1.5 Quarts
Cooking Time: 2 Hours 35 Minutes

Ingredients:

- 1 quart container full-fat plain yogurt
- ¼ teaspoon salt
- 1 cup sugar
- 2 teaspoons cinnamon
- 1 tablespoon cloves pulverized
- 1 teaspoon vanilla extract
- 1 cup strong brewed coffee or espresso
- 1 tablespoon coffee grounds

Directions:

1. NOTE: Freeze your ice cream bowl for at least 24hrs prior to starting!
2. Place the yogurt in a bowl. Use a whisk to mix in the sugar and salt. Continue to whisk for about 4 minutes until the sugar dissolves. Then mix in the vanilla extract, coffee, and coffee grounds, cloves and cinnamon.
3. Pour the ingredients into your ice cream maker, and let it churn for 25 minutes.
4. Put the frozen yogurt in an airtight container and place in the freezer for at least 2 hours, until desired consistency is reached.

Brown Sugar Honey Mango Frozen Yogurt

Servings: 1 Quart
Cooking Time: 2 Hours 35 Minutes

Ingredients:

- 1 quart container full-fat plain yogurt
- ¼ teaspoon salt
- 1 cup sugar
- 1 teaspoon vanilla extract
- 8 ounces mango
- 1/4 cup honey
- 2 tablespoons brown sugar

Directions:

1. NOTE: Freeze your ice cream bowl for at least 24hrs prior to starting!
2. Puree the strawberries in a food processor or blender.
3. Place the yogurt in a bowl. Use a whisk to mix in the sugar and salt. Continue to whisk for about 4 minutes until the sugar dissolves. Then mix in the vanilla extract, honey, brown sugar and mango puree.
4. Pour the ingredients into your ice cream maker, and let it churn for 25 minutes.
5. Put the frozen yogurt in an airtight container and place in the freezer for at least 2 hours, until desired consistency is reached.

Watermelon Sorbet

Servings: 7
Cooking Time: 15 Minutes

Ingredients:

- 1 cup sugar
- 1 cup water
- ¼ cup lemon juice
- 3 cups watermelon, peeled and seeded

Directions:

1. Place the water and sugar in a saucepan and bring to a boil over medium heat until the sugar dissolves. Remove from the heat and place in the fridge to chill for at least 3 hours.
2. Once cooled, place the water-sugar mixture into a blender and add the rest of the ingredients. Pulse until smooth.
3. Turn on the Cuisinart and pour in the mixture.
4. Churn for 10 minutes.
5. Transfer in an airtight container and freeze overnight.

Nutrition:

- InfoCalories per serving: 77; Protein: 0.4g; Carbs: 19.8g; Fat: 0.1g Sugar: 12.3g

Wonderful Watermelon Sorbet

Servings: Makes 1 Quart
Cooking Time: 2 Hours 40 Minutes

Ingredients:

- 3 1/2 cups sliced seedless watermelon
- 6 ounce chilled pineapple juice
- 3/4 cup chilled ginger ale
- ½ cup fresh lime juice
- 1/3 cup grenadine

Directions:

1. Refer to note at the beginning of the chapter about freezing bowl.
2. Puree all ingredients in a food processor or blender.
3. Pour the ingredients into your ice cream maker, and let it churn for 25-30 minutes.
4. Place in an airtight container for up to 2 hours, until desired consistency is reached.

Vanilla Ice Cream Sponge Cake

Servings: 12
Cooking Time: 25 Minutes

Ingredients:

- 1 cup cold whole milk
- ¾ cup granulated sugar
- 2 cups cold heavy cream
- 1 teaspoon vanilla extract
- 1-pound sponge cake, sliced to 1-inch thick
- 1 cup strawberry slices
- Whipped cream

Directions:

1. Put ice water in a large mixing bowl. Place a small bowl on top of the large bowl with ice. Pour cold milk and sugar into the small bowl and whisk until the sugar is dissolved. Stir in the cream and vanilla. Stir to combine.
2. Place the cold freezer bowl in the Cuisinart Ice Cream Maker. Turn on the machine and pour in the mixture. Add one package of crushed Oreos five minutes before the time ends.
3. Stop in 25 minutes until the mixture becomes soft and creamy.
4. Transfer into an air-tight container and freeze overnight.
5. In a springform pan, place slices of sponge cake.
6. Spread ice cream on top and top with strawberry slices.
7. Repeat the process until you make three layers of sponge cake, ice cream, and strawberry.
8. Top with whipped cream.
9. Place in the fridge to set for two hours.

Nutrition:

- InfoCalories per serving:281 ; Protein: 3.9g; Carbs: 38.3g; Fat: 12.7g Sugar: 20.3g

Printed in Great Britain
by Amazon

78697441R00050